Kindred Whispers

Poems of Harsh Tenderness

Himaxee Bordoloi

BookLeaf Publishing

India | USA | UK

Made with ❤ on the BookLeaf Publishing Platform
www.bookleafpub.in
www.bookleafpub.com

Dedication

To the ones who taught me the poem of life...

To my loving Maa and Deuta,
whose love shaped my spirit,
and whose voices echo in my soul.

To my siblings—dear Dada, Upakul,
and my younger one, Samudra,
whose companionship blooms like branches,
stretching wide from the same root.

To my beloved husband, Babu,
who stirs the creative flame within me,
and gives the gentle push
that sends my heart soaring.

And to my little one, my life, my poem—Rayna,
whose laughter keeps the rhythm of my days,
and whose presence is the pulse of my soul.

Preface

Kindred Whispers: Poems of Harsh Tenderness is a collection that confronts the raw edges of life — where tenderness meets critique, nostalgia blends with harsh truths, and satirical humor unearths deep social and personal reflections.

These poems explore the suffering of women under patriarchy, the fleeting beauty of childhood, the bittersweet process of aging, and the loss of nature through the lens of my daughter. They examine the chameleon-like nature of people who shift with the times, and the boastful pride of creatures who fail to recognize their fragility. Through animal imagery and sharp satire, I invite you to witness the delicate dance between the harsh and the tender, the strength and vulnerability we all carry.

This collection is both a critique and a celebration — of societal norms, of time, and of our connection to each other and the earth. It is an invitation to reflect, to laugh, to mourn, and ultimately to reconnect with the world and self we often overlook.

To my kindred spirits — those who shape my world and

my words — I dedicate these whispers. May they speak
to you with the same tenderness and truth they hold for
me.

Acknowledgements

First and foremost, I would like to express my deepest gratitude to Book Leaf, whose 21-day writing challenge ignited the spark of creativity that led to this collection. Thank you for providing the opportunity to explore and nurture my poetic voice.

A special thanks to my mother, who has been my first reader, critic, and constant source of inspiration. Her encouragement and love for poetry nurtured my passion from a young age. I am forever grateful for the seeds of creativity she planted in me.

To my father, who has always stood by my side, offering unwavering support and love, I am deeply thankful.

My siblings, whose presence has always brought joy, laughter, and a sense of belonging—thank you for your love and camaraderie.

To my husband K Babu Shankar Rao, and my child, Rayna, whose boundless love, patience, and encouragement have been my anchor throughout this journey, I dedicate my deepest thanks. You are my constant source of strength.

I am also thankful to my students at Darrang College, whose enthusiasm and curiosity inspire me to learn alongside them. Teaching them has been a reminder of the joy of discovery and the importance of nurturing creativity.

To every poet who has inspired my work—your words have shaped and enriched my journey in immeasurable ways. I carry your influence in every line I write.

I must also acknowledge nature, the greatest poet, whose company gives me warmth, comfort, and endless inspiration. The trees, the skies, the wind—they speak to me in ways words cannot capture.

I am especially grateful to the tiny creatures of the earth —ants, bees, and others—who teach me about socialization, cooperation, and the beauty of small yet essential roles in the greater whole.

And finally, I owe my acknowledgement to John Keats, my first love of poetry, whose words and spirit continue to guide and inspire me. His work remains a timeless wellspring of beauty and emotion in my own poetic life.

1. This Thing Called Patriarchy

My grandmother's arms were strong,
Gnarled from years of toil.
She walked to the field,
Her infant cradled behind her back.
"The world is a cruel song,
And I have a male child," she took pride.
She scattered the seeds—
And so did this seed called patriarchy,
Sinking deep,
Unseen but growing.

In the quiet of the night,
I meet many grandmothers.
One, *Anjakhaiti,*
Fed herself before the men.
Her hunger wasn't defiance,
But guilt overthrowing
The secret rebellion in the shadows.
"It was irresistible," she confesses in a dream,

If taste itself could be freedom.

Another, *Powiburhi,*
A fragile bird with a walking stick,
Malnourished and weary,
Spoke of her life with a sigh:
"*Bassa,* I couldn't keep myself strong,
The leftover crumbs always glorified me."
Her words, like brittle leaves, fall to the ground.
Little did she know
This thing called patriarchy

Then, there was another—
A storyteller whose voice filled the air
Like a river flowing through open skies.
Well-read, well-fed,
But barren of the fruit they longed for.
And so they named her *Baji,*
Her name a sounding echo
In my reverie.

I shall weave a thread of names.
Names half-spoken,
Lost like forgotten hymns,
Buried deeper than time's own dust,
As I lull softly,

The Matriarch's serenade,
To my daughter.

2. Beauty in Grey

I do not dread the grey sky.
It doesn't baffle me
Like the many-splendored hues
Of a blue evening.
It fills me with a joy-
Much like itself-
Plain,
Palpable,
Perspicuous.
The Knife-edged breeze,
Underneath,
Drops down the imminent tidings-
Not of the quiet April showers,
But of uprooted trees,
Painfully
Persevering
and
Persisting
The flood
Of life.

I do not dread the landscape,
of fields with grey scattered mist,
of rocky grey stones,
Sketched by my dear one.
The sharp leaden pencil,
Promises a different beauty in grey!

3. Tale of a Working Mom

I buy her crayons
But Iam afraid
She will draw a bad mom.
"Mama, will you put me to sleep, please?"
"I am sorry darling
I shall tell you a story tonight...
The story...
Yes the story...
Colourful slides...Ah...the princess...ah...frogs
croak...ahhh... Where was I?
Asleep Baby?
Dreaming already?
I am so sorry".
The Struggle is real
The Story is real
S for Stress
B for Burnout
H for Hypocrisy
M for Mockery.
Perhaps... you are too young

To understand this story.
I wish I could freeze the fleeting moments.
Don't grow up so soon.
Let me hold you in my arms
For five more minutes.
Oh! The Biometric.
I have a class...
Labels of a working mom
Make me great
or small?
I shall buy you new crayons.

4. A Queen

A Queen she was,
coronated to rule
the kingdom of his heart.
How 'royal' her days were!
Their souls united to illuminate
the darkness of divisions.
Her chores were 'our jobs'.
His stunts were 'our tasks'.
Her lively spirit
tinted with his rosy hues of love.
A Queen she was
Willing to conquer
the prejudices lurking in every mind.
But who intervened
Was the power possessed Knight.
Swarming to split her kingdom
Into two unequal halves.
Her chores were now strictly hers.
His herculean tasks his gallantry.
A Queen she is,

persevering to restore
her shattered kingdom
from the ruins of 'norms'
'dictates' and 'customs'.
A puzzle piece she is,
sometimes she fits in,
at times she drops out.
Still she ventures relentlessly
To regenerate the dismantled
masterpiece of life.

5. What ails me?

What ails me?
The burden of my own inhuman self,
A vain-glorious self who is deaf
to the pangs and sobs
of the one
pleading and wailing for life.
No *Yamdoot* had damned their souls
No devils could assign them death and hell.
Yet they cried in vain
"O spare us humans
We are humans too".
I thought I was a sojourner of this earth
feeding the fleeting moments with musings
of values sublime.
The vanity of my corporeal self
weighs heavy upon my humane self.
I lack humanity
I lack affinity.
What ails me?
The remnants of a 'self' in tattered values.

6. Love

She takes a break
from her mother's teat
A smile to her first love,
what love more profound
than an infant's glittering eyes?
she smiles, she grows, she cares, she loves.
she is loved, indeed!
sometimes she pictures
ghouls and beasts
shrieking squeaky screams.
And then she fondly recalls her father's love.
Wish he were here...
Alas!
He was a man,
moulded,
neither to receive, nor weep.
Does he dare live
with the thirty bucks
of his lady love?
Yet the Bobby printed frock of his toddler,

though time-worn
is love stained.
The rusted cycle lying
on the corner of the garage
reveberates the
ding dong dangling
of his teenage daughter.
He loved her indeed!
There was a time,
she smiled to him
to her
to them .
Now she laughs hysterically,
a mad woman in another attic.
He can't laugh STILL,
while swimming, swinging, swallowing.
who loved them in deed?

7. Of Lice and Lies

The gleaming sunshine
on the fresh mud of my grandmother's yard
radiates the hush of muffled voices.
Of women casting their faces down,
their intriguing eyes,
preying on the lice,
caught amidst the web of ther fuzzy twines.
The hallowed ground holds memories,
of turmeric scented fingers,
untangling
tresses of baby sitting
of schools unattended
of humming ached wind.
The crackling between her enticing fingers
unsounds voices
once scarcely heard.
The red-stained fingers
rewind
stories of lice and lies.

8. Bygone Childhood

The raw mangoes on my front porch
smells of a tangy childhood.
Thinly sliced mangoes, salted and savoured
with a pinch of giggling,
a shred of sharing
tasting delicious,
of love and compassion.
The golden rays of the setting sun
mirror images of a blissful childhood.
Daddy's fingers;
clasping, clingling and crossing,
the silhouette of fluttering wings:
soaring, slowing and sinking
across the horizon of my soul's lens
I yearn for those dazzling games.
Palms on the eyes,
Tickling on the forehead,
coded names.
Apples?
No...

Orange?
No...
Pineapple?
Yes, yes, yes.
When sightlessness cradled
the soft embrace of tender childhood.

9. My Little Corner

I loved that little corner,
that corner where words breathed
and beckoned me
into lands unexplored-
Fairies, sylphs, nymphs, *Ratanpur,*
and Shakespeare's black ink!
Here, it strikes a revolting Caliban,
there, it slashes Defoe's trembling hand.
I have a room of my own-
Where my daughter made her mark on the wall,
colored dotted lines of Moana, Mawi,
Rapunzel, *Champawati,* and more,
Each drawing a universe of her own.
The burden of books weighs heavy on my shelf,
and perhaps on my soul.
Crime and Punishment, The Trial-
trying the dusts of time,
unattended , unvisited, they long for me
As I long for them.
But here I lie,

Mounted on a pile of dusted papers,
swallowed by the weight of mindless anagrams,
Futile permutations and combinations
yielding nothingness.
How I miss my little corner,
where characters smeared in ink
turned filthily beautiful.

10. My Beautiful Earth

My Beautiful earth
Blend me once again
in the symphony of clay mound games,
in the dampness that nurtured my creative wings,
sprouting dreams from primordial mud.

Sway me once again
to the rhythm of grandmother's earthen lamp—
flickering laughter of toil and soil,
among dusty bullock carts.

I see no woods in my backyard today.
The muddy footprints
through the dappled sunlight
unfold the blue in bizarre boundaries.

Disavowing the drying earth,
a new territory births in silence,
where mothers, torn between duty and blood,
gift deeds with trembling hands—

a promise sealed in blue
to end the ancient feud.

My Beautiful Earth,
I scarcely fathom the gnomes
treasuring the grassy green.

Lull me once again
to thy divine cadences
of hope and healing.

11. A New Dawn

Darkling clouds stretched wide in the sky
dripping tiny drops of bestiary.
Tiny it seemed
to the unmindful eye,
now afloat in waves of misery.

Mourning smoke rose from the earth
leaving traces of
loss and death.
The illegitimate offspring
of pollution and dirt
now chokes humanity on the breath.

Etched memories flare from the fire
Flickering lessons of solidarity.
Man's hubris now rest
on the funeral pyre
paving a new dawn for humanity.

12. My last song

Cold as I lie
on this mossy ground,
pitied and condoled,
"a good soul-
a compassionate being".
My weary eye balls,
though dead and alive,
couldn't spot that tiny tear,
streaming down your anguished face.
I whisper once again,
"keep calm! It's never too late,
let us start afresh".
But in vain!
For distance,
though not of a mile now,
cannot traverse through
the empty void.
Newly clad, as I am
in this snowy white garment,
perhaps, you could see

twenty hands in unison,
readying to clear,
my blanket of pride,
my bed of ego,
my *chadar* of guilt
my robe of anger.
Weretched, as i lie
on this mound of clay,
damp, moist and still-
worms nad pests swarm in
to feast upon this nest-flesh.

13. Childhood's Fear

Sometimes my brother found my father's toothbrush
missing —
and a fluttering fear flickered in his tiny soul.
Perhaps he won't be home tonight !
And he cried clouds.
And then there were days
when the April sky screamed,
and I searched secretively for my mother's bosom
amidst the boom beast blaring.
Thankfully, we are growing older and older,
and we overcame our childhood's fear.
I teach *My mother at sixty-six* now,
and, suddenly, I realize my father is sixty-nine.
The trembling touch of my father
reminds me of his once-powerful arms,
which withstood our six little army of arms.
My mother, now hunched in silence,
seems crooked as she still cooks
a curling cabbage.
Our childhood's fear

takes shape anew
in ticking hearts
and borrowed breaths.
Wrapped in medicine bottles
and perfumed sterile—
this fear lingers still.

14. A visit to my ancestral village.

I take my daughter to my ancestral village,
To remind her that the earth still exists,
And it must be remembered.
She searches for the fox in the fields —
Stories are more real to her than reality.
I longed for my own story:
Lovers sitting at the pool's edge,
Teenagers clearing the moss-mottled fields
for play,
And sandpipers and white-winged wood ducks
reaching for the green.
But none remains.
Beyond the pond, a meadow stretches —
Where bamboo leaves sway,
holding time's secret.
We see a few youngsters,
selfie-snapping,
rushing and reeling.
The background is important, they say.

Indeed, I contemplate:
The background, now blurry,
exiled by empty echoes.
I tell my daughter,
The vixen still roams this village.
We shall find her next Bihu.

15. Once upon a time

Didst thou compare her to the radiant moon—
The very essence of beauty,
The Muse that stirs the poet's tune?

Oh! It was once—
Once upon a time...

In some forgotten woodland shade
Wandered a noble, gallant knight,
In search of she who was
So calm—yet bright.

Didst thou say she bewitched thee,
With lullabies soft and beauty rare?

Oh! It was once—
Once upon a time.

Shall thou again marvel at the light
Of the moulder—

The poet, the painter, the living sculptor?

But now—the sky bears no light.
Emptiness haunts the meadows tonight.

Naught remains but the spiteful witch
Wailing and Whining in her loathsome ditch.

Compare her not to stars nor skies;
She dwells in decay, where filth lies—
No more divine, no more sublime.

16. Time Flies

Time flies;
Traces of memory remain.

A canopy of light—
sheltering lovers
from the crackle of gunfire.

The fragrance of longing
rises from the ashes
of the fallen—
drifting far, far away,
to where the true God dwells—
not the one in whose name
blood stains the Chinar,
parting lovers
like rivers forced to split.

Time flies;
Traces of memory remain.

Coy smiles
framed behind glass,
vermilion laughter—
soft, trembling—
echoes of promises
painted in rose-hued light.

Time flies;
Traces of memory remain.

The placenta of love,
nurturing the embryonic pulse
of another life,
still forming,
still dreaming.

17. Chameleons

In childhood,
I saw a chameleon.
Its skin shimmered in soft greens and gold.
I whispered, "It's beautiful."

My mother said,
"Be careful—
snakes and lizards may hiss,
but a color-changing chameleon
can be far more dangerous."

Her words,
like old proverbs,
settled gently on my young mind.
I didn't understand—
not yet.

I grew up
among reptiles:
some cold,

some loud,
some with teeth always bared.
They hissed to my face,
they whispered behind my back—
but their nature was clear.
They meant what they showed.

Then came the others.

The ones with smiles painted on shifting skin,
words wrapped in warmth
but laced with venom.
They praised with one color,
envied in another,
and vanished in silence
when storms loomed.

Now I see chameleons again—
not in trees,
but in boardrooms,
in gossips,
in friendships,
in fleeting alliances.

Shifting shades—
from sympathy to spite,
from empathy to ego,

puffing up pride like armor,
then disappearing in plain sight.

And suddenly,
my mother's words echo back—
clearer, sharper:
Not all who change are growing.
Not all who blend belong.

Some stay silent.
Some are blunt.
The one in nature—
still harmless. But...

it's the camouflaged chameleons
that strike us most.

18. The Boasting Beasts

Some animals once claimed a grand feat,
With boasts they felt were quite sweet.
But one by one, as you'll soon see,
Their true selves were set free.

A brown frog was making
Bombastic croaking.
Little sense did it make
To his friends in the lake,
And they said, "He's faking, he's faking."

A puffed-up fox went out for prey,
Disguised in a lion-like display.
He slipped in the mud,
With a thud-thud-thud,
And lay there, exposed in the clay.

A dog raised a ruckus with might,
Till a bone made him hush with delight.
Another one growled,

With sharp teeth he scowled—
He could hardly bite, just fight.

Now, each of these creatures, full of flair,
Found their pretensions caught in the air.
For in the end, it's clear to see:
True strength lies in humility.

19. The Conclusion

Perhaps the conclusion is the hardest part—
gathering fragments of friendships
formed in the inebriated sea
of rose-tinted love,
solitude, ambition, hope,
and the quiet shadow of disease.

Shades of grey
drifted back and forth
on Keats' wings of poesy,
across Whitman's weathered deck;
though thousands lay—
choked and breathless—
O Captain!

Which deity answers now?

There were conversations—
through digital windows,
and sometimes across a table,

when eyes held a certain fire.

Stories emerged,
summoning Jane,
Faustus,
Foucault,
Derrida—

Unapologetically true,
even when brushed with blasphemy.

Now, a chapter closes.

The conclusion, perhaps, is difficult—
but deeply significant.

20. Bordoisila

It's been long since you last
combed your cloudy-curls
across your mother's home.
They say you came cruel—
with torrents tumbling,
winds wailing,
snapping poles and,
tearing through tin and bamboo,
ripping roofs from resting heads.
You stirred the spring,
made it bitter-sweet—
a storm in silk.
But it was always your ritual,
your seasonal return.
Mother threw the *peera*
and the comb,
her silent summons.
And I—
I saw the skies soften,
your fury fold into drizzle.

It's been long,
long since I saw you last.
You seemed cruel—
but beautiful,
O breathless, brooding *Bordoisila*.
Our *peeras* now wear cushions.
The hearth holds no fire—
only framed photos,
and a bamboo roof
shrunk to a showpiece
in the showroom of our drawing room.
The tip-tap tale
of rain on tin
is a forgotten lullaby.
The hills have hunched into memories.
The green's gone grey.
But it was always your custom
to visit your mother,
O *Bordoisila*.
What keeps you from us?
What grudge grows
in your gusty heart?
Come again—
even if cruel.
Shake the shutters,
shout through the trees.
Come and drench the dust

of our swollen egos.

** *Bordoisila* is the Assamese storm-wind spirit of spring.
** *Peera* is a traditional low wooden stool used in
Assamese households.

21. I am no Magi

I am no Magi to bring you gifts,
Though the stars are as splendid
As the night when you were first brought into this
world.
I have no silken threads from Arabia to offer,
No gold to uphold your sacred pillars,
No rubies or sapphires for your monumental temple.
I hold no VVIP pass
To catch even a fleeting glimpse of you.

But I bring a tapestry—
Woven not of silk,
But of compassion, devotion,
And selfless love.

I wish I could undertake that arduous journey
To your snow-capped dwelling,
Through mountainous terrain
And steep, echoing valleys.
Perhaps even the sore-footed yaks

Would have grunted to a halt—
And I would have carried to you
Gold, frankincense, and myrrh.

But I am no Magi to bring you gifts.
Only a pilgrim soul—
Hunched, hollow, and humbled.
I can barely fold my trembled hands
or prostrate-
Yet my operated heart longs for you
and others like you,
who, like distant stars,
Burn with the quiet desire
To bridge the broken.